HiSPANiC STAR

SELENA GOMEZ

D1410464

THE HISPANIC STAR SERIES

Read about the most groundbreaking, iconic Hispanic heroes who have shaped our culture and the world in this gripping biography series for young readers.

IF YOU CAN SEE IT, YOU CAN BE IT.

SELENA GOMEZ

CLAUDIA ROMO EDELMAN
AND **KARLA ARENAS VALENTI**

ILLUSTRATED BY **ALEXANDRA BEGUEZ**

ROARING BROOK PRESS

NEW YORK

Published by Roaring Brook Press
Roaring Brook Press is a division of Holtzbrinck Publishing Holdings Limited
Partnership
120 Broadway, New York, NY 10271 • mackids.com

Written by Claudia Romo Edelman and Karla Arenas Valenti.
Illustrated by Alexandra Beguez.

Our books may be purchased in bulk for promotional, educational, or business
use. Please contact your local bookseller or the Macmillan Corporate and
Premium Sales Department at (800) 221–7945 ext. 5442 or by email at
MacmillanSpecialMarkets@macmillan.com.

Library of Congress Control Number: 2022916321

First edition, 2023
Book design by Julia Bianchi
Printed in the United States of America by Lakeside Book Company, Harrisonburg,
Virginia

ISBN 978-1-250-82831-6 (paperback)
10 9 8 7 6 5 4 3 2 1

ISBN 978-1-250-82830-9 (hardcover)
10 9 8 7 6 5 4 3 2 1

For my mom,
who lost her battle to Covid, but whose
values live in me every day. I am who I am because
she was the best of role models.

For my husband, Richard, and children, Joshua and
Tamara, who surround me with their love,
their belief in me, and support.
They make it all possible.

Most of all, this series is dedicated to
the children of tomorrow. We know that you
have to see it to be it.
We hope these Latino heroes teach you to
spread your wings and fly.
—C. R. E.

To you, reader—may you find in this Hispanic
Star a kindred spirit.
—K. A. V.

CHAPTER ONE

SMALL-TOWN GIRL

"We knew we wanted her as a star."

—GARY MARSH, president of entertainment
for Disney Channels Worldwide

It's raining in a small town between Fort Worth and Dallas, Texas. The water gathers in puddles outside a house in Grand Prairie, number 205, where Selena Gomez knocks on a white door and waits.

This is the home she grew up in.

Plink-Plonk-Plink

Raindrops fall onto the mailbox, sliding off the side and adding to the wet patch on the grass.

Plip-Plop-Plip

The rain splatters onto the cement steps leading up to the door.

Selena recalls putting her hands into the wet cement on

the sidewalk when she was five. She remembers her nana sitting with friends, listening to music and sipping iced tea.

"I visit this place every chance I get," she says, and explains how she used to splash around the yard during rainstorms just like this one. And when it wasn't raining, "it smelled like fresh-cut grass."

Selena may have left this home, but it is still very much a part of her. She knocks a second time, but it's clear nobody is home.

Selena's mother, Mandy Teefey, has some Italian ancestry, and her father, Ricardo Joel Gomez, is of Mexican descent. Both were sixteen when Selena was born, and her mother gave up everything to support her daughter.

"We didn't have a lot growing up," Selena says.

Her grandparents helped take care of her while her parents finished their schooling. Family meant everything to them, and they were willing to do whatever they could to support Selena and her parents.

But raising a child at such a young age was difficult for Mandy and Joel. It put a tremendous strain on their marriage, until the marriage fell apart when Selena was five. Her mom and dad divorced, and Selena stayed with her mother. Her mom struggled to make ends meet, living paycheck to paycheck and working multiple jobs at a time to provide for her daughter.

"She was really strong around me," Selena says. "Having me at sixteen had to have been a big responsibility. She gave up everything for me, had three jobs, supported me, sacrificed her life for me. My mom was always doing a hundred million things just to make me happy."

And Selena *was* happy. She was surrounded by love and a family that supported her. But the person Selena has become is a woman forged by more than a happy childhood. She is no stranger to the challenges of transformation, the struggle of finding who you are and living that truth. And it is precisely that effort that makes Selena the star she is today.

Born on July 22, 1992, Selena Marie Gomez began her life in Grand Prairie, Texas, a city with a population of close to 200,000 people. Almost half the population is of Hispanic or Latinx descent.

Every year, the town hosts Prairie Lights, a two-mile-long winter attraction with more than three hundred million lights. For forty days, angels, elves, penguins, reindeer, snowmen, stars, the world's longest tunnel of lights, and hundreds of others features are on display as part of this very unique holiday experience.

Another claim to fame for Grand Prairie are some of

SELENA QUINTANILLA PÉREZ was a Grammy Award–winning Tejano music superstar who rose to fame in the early 1990s. Born on April 16, 1971, in Lake Jackson, Texas, Selena Quintanilla's musical talent was evident by the age of six. When the family relocated to Corpus Christi, Selena Quintanilla and her father, Abraham Quintanilla Jr., formed Selena y Los Dinos, the band that led to Selena Quintanilla's meteoric rise to fame.

A native of Texas, Selena Quintanilla became known as the "Queen of Tejano Music"—Tejano music is also known as Tex-Mex music—a style that fused Mexican norteño music with European and US influences, distinguished primarily by orchestration and usually featuring the accordion as lead instrument. Selena Quintanilla also became a fashion icon, developing a signature style that cemented her as the "Tejano Madonna." Beloved by many, Selena's legacy and impact remains strong, almost thirty years after her untimely and tragic death in 1995.

the best national parks and recreation venues in the area. That and, of course, being the birthplace of Selena!

Her parents named her after one of their favorite singers: Selena.

Like her namesake, Selena Gomez would go on to become one of the most influential Latinx artists of all time. Though young Selena Gomez didn't know it then, she was just starting off on her extraordinary journey.

As a young girl, Selena was always sensitive, thoughtful, and kind. She was also fearless, never shying away from doing what she thought was right or from helping others, even when *she* was afraid.

Her capacity for empathy was captured perfectly in a photograph taken for the local Grand Prairie paper.

It was Selena's first day of preschool, a day of great hopes and expectations, fears, and tearful goodbyes. Colorful cutouts adorned the walls; books eagerly awaited the hands of little children; crayons and scissors and glue were ready to create epic art projects.

Selena's heart beat wildly as she prepared to embark on this new adventure. She took a breath, grinned, and bid her mom goodbye, stepping valiantly into the new classroom. Off to the side and all alone sat a tearful child, a fellow classmate who was not quite as fearless as young Selena.

Flash!

A camera captured the scene: little Selena offering comfort to another who shared her fears and needed a friend to lean on. In a time of great change and uncertainty, Selena was able to reach out to friends who needed her strength and comfort.

As Selena grew up, she found different ways to offer comfort to those less fortunate than her.

Even though Selena and her mom had so little, "I remember always being reminded that people had less than we did," Selena says. "My mom would run out of gas all of the time, and we'd sit there and have to go through the car and get quarters and help her get gas." Or they would have to walk to the dollar store to get dollar spaghetti for dinner.

Yet, despite their own fragile situation, Selena and her mom would volunteer at soup kitchens on Thanksgiving and regularly go through her closet to find clothes to donate.

The habit of kindness and goodwill toward others that began when Selena was a young girl has become a defining feature of Selena as an adult—guiding her through the many trials and tribulations she has encountered throughout her thirty years.

Back in the white house in Grand Prairie, Selena explains that her interest in acting was first inspired by watching her mom prepare for theater productions as a stage actress in Dallas. Selena's dad was a DJ, so as a child, she was always surrounded by creativity. This instilled in her a deep love of performing arts.

It didn't take long for her love to transform the family living room into a lively stage where Selena would host concert performances or beauty pageants for her family. But soon, what started as small family-only performances evolved into auditioning for various TV roles . . .

And the opportunity of a lifetime!

Barney & Friends was a hit children's television series that launched in 1992. The series' star was Barney, a friendly purple dinosaur who taught important educational and moral concepts.

The series also featured a green triceratops, Baby Bop, and her brother, BJ, a yellow protoceratops. The dinosaurs interacted with a number of adult characters, such as Mother Goose, along with more than one hundred children who appeared as guests over the course of fourteen seasons.

Lights!

Camera!

Action!

Every episode of the show began with a group of kids playing together and imagining that Barney—a cute stuffed animal—would magically come to life as a real dinosaur. Barney and the other dinosaur friends would then delve into a specific topic or theme to be explored that day through songs and dance with the guest children and adult actors.

Beloved by many, *Barney & Friends* taught viewers many important social and emotional skills. For example, early episodes talked about different ways children can use their imagination and what makes families so wonderful. Some episodes dealt with more practical matters, such as safety when crossing streets or talking to strangers. The show even ventured into conversations about how to be healthy, how to navigate complicated emotions, and how to deal with challenging personal situations.

As luck would have it, *Barney & Friends* filmed in Carrollton, a suburb near Dallas and just a thirty-minute drive from Grand Prairie.

TALENT SEARCH!

Representatives for Barney & Friends *are looking for young talent to join the show. If you are a boy or girl between the ages of 10 and 17 years old and you are interested in acting, singing, or dancing, please contact us for more information!*

When Selena was ten, she answered a casting call to be one of the show's child actors. At the audition she met Demi Lovato.

DEMI LOVATO is a singer, songwriter, and actor born on August 20, 1992. Like Selena, they got their start on *Barney & Friends* and rose to fame after starring as aspiring musician Mitchie Torres in the Disney Channel Original Movie *Camp Rock.*

Selena and Demi tried out for a guest spot on the show, and both were selected to appear in the series in 2002. Selena would portray the character of Gianna, a young girl of Mexican-Italian descent, very similar to her own background.

In Selena's first episode as Gianna, she, Barney, and BJ teach Baby Bop about proper manners. In another episode, the friends direct traffic, teaching viewers about *stop* and *go*. Other episodes with Gianna taught children about instruments, seasons, sharing, and the importance of friends and family. In the very last episode in which Selena portrayed Gianna, the friends celebrated Barney's birthday.

Being on *Barney & Friends* was a huge change for Selena, a young performer who had never before done any professional acting and knew very little about the film and television industry. Up until then, she had only ever watched her mother perform in community theater. But Selena embraced this new role with a fierce curiosity to learn and the courage to grow, appearing in thirteen episodes of *Barney & Friends* between 2002 and 2004 (during the show's seventh and eighth seasons).

Perhaps most people would have felt intimidated under these circumstances, stressed by the long hours and demanding schedule of working on a show like this. But not Selena. Her passion for acting, and her fearless ability to embrace new things, made her feel as if this wasn't even work.

For her it was a blast! "You're on set with a big purple dinosaur and dancing and having a great time," she said in an interview.

During the two years Selena starred on *Barney & Friends*, she learned everything she could about acting and the TV and film industry. She also continued auditioning for other roles and eventually landed a small speaking role in the film *Spy Kids 3-D: Game Over,* as well as guest starring in various other TV programs.

KINDS OF ROLES IN FILM AND TELEVISION

In film and television, there are different jobs an actor can have and receive credit for. Some of these include:

- **BACKGROUND TALENT:** This refers to performers, also called extras, who appear in the background and help give the scene a more realistic feel. They typically have very small, non-speaking roles.
- **DAY PLAYER:** These are actors with few speaking parts and who only appear in one or two scenes. For example, a day player could be someone who is being interviewed by a main character.

- SERIES REGULAR: A series regular is part of the main cast for a show, contracted to work for a specific period of time (which can be a month or multiple years) on a show. They are considered to be part of the main storyline, so their character is important. However, that doesn't mean they will appear in every episode.
- RECURRING: These are performers who appear in multiple episodes in a single season or throughout the whole series. They are not necessarily a main character or series regular, but they appear more frequently than a day player.
- GUEST STAR: A guest star is a well-known actor who appears in a show as a special performance. They usually appear in one (or only a few) episodes, and their characters often play an important role in the storyline.
- CAMEO: A cameo refers to a brief appearance or voice performance by a well-known actor in a show or movie.

Then, when she was ten, Selena attended a nationwide Disney talent search. With lines upon lines of talented actors from across the country—everyone eager for a shot at their dream—it's easy to get discouraged and lose hope.

But Selena was not at all discouraged. She leaped at the opportunity and auditioned.

Auditioning for a role like this can be very nerve-racking. You are standing by yourself on a stage with blinding lights cast upon you. A group of very important TV or film executives are there to evaluate you. Sometimes you can see them sitting before you; sometimes they're in a booth and out of sight.

You're given a scene and a role to play. Depending on the audition, you may have a set of lines to practice in advance. But often you are asked to improvise.

For example, someone might say, "Pretend you are at school and you realize you forgot to do your homework. You have to come up with a good excuse for your teacher." Then you have to act out the scene, right then and there.

If the executives like your performance, they'll call you back to do another audition, maybe with other characters from the show or people they are considering casting. Usually you have to go through many auditions, and only a few make it to the very end.

Selena was a natural. Her charm and charismatic appeal were an instant win, and she made it through each of the auditions and all the way to the final casting call.

What was the role?

Selena was cast in an episode of *The Suite Life of*

Zack & Cody, a series centered on twin brothers Zack and Cody Martin, who live in the Tipton Hotel in Boston, where their mother is a performer in the hotel lounge.

This role was not her first time acting on TV. But it was another first for Selena because in the show, Selena's character shared a kiss with Zack during the school play.

WHAT'S A PILOT EPISODE?

A TV PILOT is a standalone episode that a producer will film to show TV executives from a network—like Disney Channel—what a new show will be like.

First, what does a producer actually do?

For every show, the producer is in charge of hiring a director, the crew, the cast, the scriptwriters, and making sure the show is produced, or created. However, the people who decide if a show is actually good enough to air on cable TV or streaming services are the network executives.

So creating a pilot and pitching a show that is good enough to convince network executives is a pretty big deal!

A kiss!

Filmed in front of the whole cast!

And all the camera crew!

And the director!

And her parents!

Selena was very nervous. Especially since this was her very first kiss, and it would be on-screen for the whole world to see! Fortunately Selena was a natural in front of the camera. The scene went flawlessly, and the episode was a success.

Soon after, Selena was invited to film a pilot episode for a spin-off of *The Suite Life of Zack & Cody* for a series titled *Arwin!*

Arwin! was pitched as a show about the Tipton Hotel's handyman, a man named Arwin who moves in with his sister to help take care of her kids. Selena had been cast to play one of those children.

After the episode was filmed and the producers took it to the network executives, they waited to hear the verdict . . .

And waited . . .

And waited!

Unfortunately, the pilot episode didn't quite convince the executives at Disney, who decided not to move forward with the show. This might have slowed other rising performers down. But it did not stop Selena!

In 2007 she was cast in another role, this time as Mikayla Skeech—a rival pop star to Miley Cyrus's character Hannah on the hit show *Hannah Montana*.

Hannah Montana followed fourteen-year-old Miley Stewart, an ordinary girl who seems to live a normal life but has a secret identity as pop star Hannah Montana. In the series, "Hannah Montana" is an alias chosen by Miley and her family so she can keep her private life separate from the public spotlight.

On *Hannah Montana*, Mikayla and Hannah are pop star enemies. But when Mikayla meets Miley, not knowing she is actually Hannah Montana, they become fast friends. This storyline created an interesting conflict, which made this a recurring role for Selena. It also gave her a chance to show the producers and executives at Disney what she was capable of doing. This certainly helped when Selena auditioned for, and ultimately landed, the role coveted by hundreds of applicants who auditioned: Alex Russo on Disney Channel's new series *Wizards of Waverly Place*.

This role changed everything for Selena, skyrocketing her career.

"We knew we wanted her as a star in the Disney Channel universe," said Gary Marsh, president of entertainment for Disney Channels Worldwide.

Wizards of Waverly Place was a fantasy teen sitcom revolving around Alex as a teenage wizard living in Manhattan with her Italian-Mexican-American family. Together with her siblings, Justin and Max, they undertake wizard training, knowing that one day they will compete to win sole custody of their family's wizarding powers. The series had heavy elements of fantasy and magic, but its principal theme was one of family, friendship, and the challenges of growing up.

It was also one of the first series that featured a Latinx lead character, incorporating Mexican culture and Spanish language into some of the episodes. This did not go unnoticed by a growing Latinx viewership who helped boost the show's ratings. It also gave many viewers a window into what it was like for Hispanic and Latinx families growing up in the United States at that time.

The show was a tremendous success, winning multiple awards and cementing Selena as a rising star, with fans not only in Texas but also all across the United States and even around the world.

With her Hollywood career on the rise, it became quite difficult to manage everything while living so far from the heart of the action. So Selena and her mom understood it was time to say goodbye to Grand Prairie, Texas. They packed up the white house and moved to Los Angeles, California, where Selena would begin the next phase of her life.

As the rain continues to fall on the white house in Grand Prairie, Selena takes a photo. "I love you, Grand Prairie," she says, opening her umbrella and stepping down onto the puddle-full sidewalk. "Thank you!"

CHAPTER TWO

GROWING UP IN THE SPOTLIGHT

"Gomez is a master at being the annoying, selfish Alex, and her portrayal of a typical 16-year-old rings entirely true."

—ROXANA HADADI, Express contributor
for The Washington Post

Becoming a Disney protégée was a dream come true in many ways for Selena. *Wizards of Waverly Place* was one of the most viewed shows in the United States on broadcast television. It spawned soundtrack albums, merchandising, and even a video game adaptation.

The themes of fantasy and secret identities had tremendous appeal for the audience, but so did the stories that centered around family, friends, and growing up.

In the series, Alex grew up in a mixed-race working-class family that revered familial heritage, hard work, and honoring one's responsibilities. These values spoke to many viewers growing up in similar families and backgrounds.

And fans especially loved Selena's character, Alex: an edgy, tomboyish teen, similar to Selena's own style at the time.

Filming for the show took place in Hollywood Center Studios, the world-famous studio, where a set was built to resemble a New York apartment. The first episode aired on October 12, 2007. After four seasons, the series finale aired on January 6, 2012, and had achieved so much popularity that it was the most-watched finale episode of any Disney Channel show.

Selena was praised for her performance, and *Wizards of Waverly Place* brought her a great deal of recognition and acclaim. Disney began marketing her as one of its biggest stars.

And not just for her acting.

Selena's music career was about to take off.

In addition to starring in the series, Selena recorded the theme song for *Wizards of Waverly Place*, "Everything Is Not What It Seems." She also began appearing in music videos, including a video for the Jonas Brothers' song "Burnin' Up."

Selena was invited to contribute a cover of the song "Cruella De Vil," which was a part of the 2008 *Disneymania*

6 album compilation, along with a number of other well-known musicians, including her best friend from their *Barney & Friends* days, Demi Lovato.

Selena later recorded a song for the soundtrack of the animated film *Tinker Bell*. That same year she recorded three songs for the soundtrack to the movie *Another Cinderella Story*, in which she also played the lead role as aspiring dancer Mary Santiago.

As if that wasn't enough, her musical talent extended to voice acting, where she voiced the role of Helga in the animated film *Horton Hears a Who!*

Horton Hears a Who! is the movie adaptation of Dr. Seuss's popular book of the same name. The book tells the story of Horton, an elephant, and his adventures in Whoville, a tiny planet located on a speck of dust. Helga is one of the daughters of the mayor of Whoville.

The movie was released in 2008 and was a tremendous international success, further launching Selena into the limelight. The world was paying attention to this Disney star, but Selena was not daunted.

As fearlessly as she tackled her first day at preschool, she dove into her burgeoning voice acting and musical career. At the age of sixteen, Selena signed a record deal with Hollywood Records, the Disney Music Group record label that had signed other Hollywood stars like Miley Cyrus and Demi Lovato.

Using the power of the Disney enterprise, Hollywood Records was able to very successfully establish Selena as a musical pop star. Her first real entry into this world came with the pop rock band she formed in 2008 called Selena Gomez & the Scene.

Forming a band and recording an album requires a huge commitment and great deal of passion, as well as a tremendous amount of work. Selena put as much of her mind, heart, and soul into this project as she did into all her other initiatives.

She was very diligent and deliberate in the audition process, looking for musicians who were passionate about making music and could "seriously rock out." In 2009, after many hours spent auditioning and writing and practicing and recording and rerecording . . . Selena Gomez & the Scene debuted their studio album *Kiss & Tell*.

Imagine what that must have been like.

Have you ever poured your heart and mind into something that was so important to you that you forgot about everything else? You worked so hard, you gave up so many things, and you are probably really proud of how it turned out. More than anything else, you want other people to love what you made as much as you do.

Selena Gomez & the Scene felt the same way.

The band waited to see what people thought.

What if listeners didn't like it?

What if people thought the music was terrible?

What if people criticized the singing?

Well, that's exactly what happened. Many listeners did not like the album; they thought the music was bad, and others were very critical of Selena's singing.

But Selena did not let this defeat her. She knew there were other voices in the fray, fans and not just her critics.

And she was right.

Kiss & Tell went on to sell more than 500,000 copies. It topped music charts all over the world. Fans in Greece, Poland, and the United Kingdom loved her work so much they launched the album to the Top 40. The band was on fire!

Selena Gomez & the Scene promoted the album on a concert tour, traveling for almost a year all across the United States: from California to Texas to New York and back. They even toured in London, England. Selena Gomez & the Scene also made various televised performances, and they appeared on many shows to promote their album.

It was demanding and exhausting work. The band was

forced to spend a great deal of time away from home and with very few breaks. Nevertheless, they didn't pass up any opportunities to connect with fans. In addition to touring, they also contributed to Disney's *All Wrapped Up Vol. 2* album compilation and continued making their own new music.

That year, Selena Gomez & the Scene recorded a number of hit singles and music videos, including the band's biggest single to date. "Naturally" has sold more than a million copies in the United States! The song's lyrics capture a theme that has come to define the young star: Stay true to yourself.

How you choose to express yourself . . .
You follow what you feel inside

In 2010 the band released their second studio album, *A Year Without Rain.*

"I'm really proud of this record," Selena said in an interview. "I wanted to make sure it made people feel good, but I also dedicated a couple songs to my fans, because there were moments onstage that I wish I could give to them, because they mean so much to me."

Unfortunately, as with her first record, it received mixed

reviews, with some critics complaining about the effects applied to Selena's vocals. Nevertheless, the album debuted at number four and sold more than 500,000 copies in the United States. A Spanish version of the single title track "A Year Without Rain" ("Un Año Sin Lluvia") was released three months after the English version.

For the next year, Selena and her band were very busy promoting their music on TV, going on concert tours, and delivering live performances. They got to see all sorts of new places, adoring fans met them everywhere they went, and they were doing work they loved. It was all very exciting!

Selena had established herself as an international icon and was now in high demand! But her successful music career with Selena Gomez & the Scene was not the only thing keeping her busy. Selena was still working on *Wizards of Waverly Place*, and she continued to star in a number of other Disney shows and original movies, including *Wizards of Waverly Place: The Movie*, which won an Emmy for Outstanding Children's Program.

She reprised her role as Alex Russo in a special Disney Channel crossover event that spanned three episodes across *Wizards of Waverly Place*, *Hannah Montana*, and *The Suite Life on Deck*—a spin-off of *The Suite Life of Zack and Cody* with the twins attending classes at Seven Seas High School on the SS *Tipton*.

Selena also guest starred as herself on a series called *Sonny with a Chance*, in which her old friend Demi Lovato starred as Sonny, a teenage girl who becomes a cast member of her favorite sketch comedy TV show.

Selena and Demi also played the lead characters—best friends, Carter and Rosalinda—in the hit movie *Princess Protection Program*. The movie followed a young princess, Rosie (Demi), whose small country is invaded by a dictator and who is taken into custody by the Princess Protection Program. Rosie is whisked

THE COMMONWEALTH OF PUERTO RICO

Princess Protection Program was filmed in Puerto Rico. THE COMMONWEALTH OF PUERTO RICO (which means "rich port" in Spanish) is an archipelago in the Caribbean and an unincorporated territory of the United States. That means Puerto Rico is under the jurisdiction of the United States; the people have certain fundamental and constitutional rights but not all the same rights as an incorporated territory (like the US states). For example, all US citizens—including Puerto Ricans—can travel freely between the archipelago and the US mainland. However, Puerto Ricans cannot vote in US elections, and since they are not a state, they do not have representation in Congress.

Puerto Rico is a place of immense beauty with a rich history and culture, beautiful beaches of sapphire blue and golden sand, emerald green vegetation dotted with jewel-like flowers and fruits, and breathtaking mountains.

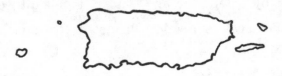

away to rural Louisiana, where she must learn to live like an ordinary American teenager. Rosie's new friend and roommate, Carter (Selena), receives a few lessons of her own from Rosie on royal etiquette and proper manners.

In addition to their hit performances in the movie, Selena and Demi also recorded "One and the Same," the promotional single for the movie.

During her time in beautiful Puerto Rico, Selena noticed there were many stray dogs and cats roaming the city streets. Her heart went out to the abandoned creatures, and she wanted to help in any way she could. Selena soon

DOSOMETHING.ORG is the largest not-for-profit exclusively for young people and social change. DoSomething's members represent the United States and 131 countries. DoSomething members join volunteer, social change, and civic action campaigns for causes they care about.

Some of their campaigns include "Teens for Jeans" (donating more than one million pairs of jeans to homeless teens in a single year); voter registration initiatives; campaigns on climate justice and mental health; collections of food donations; and Celebrate Pride! (creating the largest crowdsourced LGBTQ+ ally guide).

got involved with Island Dog Inc., a volunteer group that helps animals in Puerto Rico. She used her social media presence to encourage people to support the organization. Selena also participated in an online charity auction, the proceeds of which went to benefit Island Dog Inc. and the work they were doing in Puerto Rico.

Later, and as a result of her involvement with Island Dog Inc., Selena became the ambassador of DoSomething.org, a nonprofit youth-led movement with millions of members around the world.

Between her volunteer work, acting, and creating music, it would seem Selena had little time for anything else.

But that wasn't quite true. In 2008 Selena and her mom had formed a production company called July Moon Productions. The name was inspired by the word *selena*, which means "moon" in Greek, and her birth month (July). Owning her own production company gave Selena the ability to expand her creativity in a new way by producing her own TV and film content: selecting scripts, hiring writers, and creating talent packages.

Selena officially became a "triple threat"—a performer who excels at three performance arts. And she didn't stop there!

In 2010 Selena launched Dream Out Loud, a fashion line of eco-friendly, boho-style clothing for young girls.

"With my line, I really want to give the customers options on how they can put their own looks together," Selena said in an interview. "I want the pieces that can be easy to dress up or down, and the fabrics being eco-friendly and organic are super important."

In 2011 Selena began developing her own fragrance.

"I have three favorite smells in the world: raspberry, vanilla, and freesia," Selena explained in an interview. "Vanilla just makes me feel cozy and yummy. Raspberry is fun without being too sweet. I love how feminine freesia is. It was important to me that anyone who smelled it found it enticing."

Creating a fragrance is a long process of identifying key scents that will be the heart of the fragrance, the base, and the top notes. Over the course of six months, Selena and her team narrowed down the combinations to about seventy possibilities. Selena tested each one.

"This first one is fruity," she said as she assessed the first option. "Almost overwhelmingly so. And this second one smells like detergent. It smells clean and nice. But is it special enough?"

A third option was a closer fit: "Clean, like the second option, but with a touch of fruit—it's flirty and delicious. I love this."

Eventually she settled on her signature scent, a fruity floral fragrance called Selena Gomez Eau de Parfum. The heart of the perfume is purple freesia, musk, and dewberry. The top notes are raspberry, peach, and pineapple, and the base is chocolate, vanilla, and amber.

Creating a signature scent was not the only thing keeping Selena busy. That same year, she starred in the film *Monte Carlo*, where she played the role of a teenager mistaken for a socialite while on a trip to Paris. To prepare for the role, Selena had to learn to play polo and speak in two different British accents.

In addition to continuing to appear in a number of Disney shows, she was regularly recording music with her band. That year, they released their third and final album, *When the Sun Goes Down*, again with mixed reviews. The following year, Selena decided to step away from the band.

In 2012 *Wizards of Waverly Place* aired its finale. The last episode, "Who Will Be the Family Wizard?" was the 106th episode of the series. In it, Alex and her brothers, Justin and Max, face a sudden and ultimate test to determine who will be the one to keep their wizarding powers. They enter the final round of the competition, a massive labyrinth. The first sibling to come out of the maze will be the winner. 9.8 million viewers tuned in to find out who it would be. This episode would go down in history as the

most watched series finale for Disney Channel and the third most watched episode on the network to date.

The culmination of *Wizards of Waverly Place* was the end of an era for Selena, but things did not slow down for her at all. She soon began recording as the voice of Mavis on *Hotel Transylvania*; she starred in more films and even recorded a solo album.

In 2013 she released the lead single "Come & Get It," which became an instant hit, from her first solo album, *Stars Dance*, which also came out in 2013. It debuted at number one on the US Billboard 200 chart. It sold 97,000 copies in its first week!

Despite the album's obvious appeal, music critics complained that Selena's sound lacked an authentic musical identity. And in a way, this hinted at something deeper and more troubling that had begun to unfold in Selena's life. For, despite being surrounded by all the things she loved, Selena appeared to be losing herself.

With everything happening so quickly, Selena the person had inadvertently become "Selena" the brand: a talented actress, a gifted musician, a famous producer. She had millions of fans and followers, and her brand was incredibly valuable. This meant that with every new project she took on, Selena had to be mindful of protecting her brand image. This created a great deal of pressure: She had to ensure everything she did was as successful as everything else she had previously done. She had to make sure that nothing hindered the Selena Gomez brand in any way.

To achieve this, however, Selena had to be flawless.

"That was my job in a way," she said in an interview. "To be perfect. You're considered a figure kids look up to, and [Disney] takes that seriously."

Selena took it seriously, too, doing everything in her power to live up to that perfect image, trying so hard to please everyone, even if it didn't feel authentic. Even if it meant losing herself.

"I think I spent so many years just trying to say the right thing to people for the sake of keeping myself sane. I lost sight of who I was."

She tried to be the person others wanted her to be. But living up to those unrealistic expectations was too much. It was an impossible ask. Selena's physical and mental health began to suffer.

Selena kept pushing herself . . .

And struggling . . .

And pushing herself . . .

And suffering . . .

Until one day in 2013 when, after performing more than fifty concerts in North America and Europe as part of her *Stars Dance* tour, Selena was completely burned out. She simply could not continue at such a frenzied pace, burdened by so many unrealistic expectations.

So Selena made the very difficult decision to cancel the Australian and Asian legs of the tour. But canceling the tour was not something she took lightly. Selena loved performing, and she had an incredible work ethic. The thought of backing out of her commitments was devasting. More important, she hated disappointing her fans, and she knew they would be disappointed.

But Selena had to face the truth and accept that she was burned out.

"I knew I couldn't go on unless I learned to listen to my body and mind when I really needed help."

The following year, it was reported that Selena had voluntarily checked into a mental health facility in Arizona.

The press jumped on this, speculating about what drove Selena to make this decision, saying all number of things that painted a portrait of a falling star. Some media outlets even went so far as to suggest that Selena needed rehab because of problems with drugs and alcohol abuse. But none of that was true.

But, instead of giving herself the grace and time she needed to heal, she continued working, doing everything she could to live up to the brand she had built and show people that she wasn't failing.

Selena signed on to star in more films. Unfortunately, strained as she was, her films were met with critical reviews. She recorded more music, but her music was failing to connect with fans. At that point, Selena no longer felt that her record label was a good partnership, and in 2014, she cut ties with Hollywood Records.

Things felt like they were crumbling all around her, and Selena desperately needed some positive news, something to inspire her and help her feel hopeful. Instead, that same year she received the worst possible news: She was diagnosed with lupus, a chronic autoimmune disease that was slowly attacking her body.

Lupus is a condition in which a person's immune system can't tell the difference between foreign substances that are invading the body and their own healthy cells. So the immune system creates antibodies that mistakenly attack the healthy tissues and organs.

Because the body is attacking itself, patients often experience fevers and various aches and bodily pain, stiffness, or swelling. They are generally exhausted from the fighting going on inside them. Sometimes, their organs stop working properly. It can be very difficult to live with lupus.

THE BATTLE OF THE
IMMUNE SYSTEM

Your iMMUNe SYSTeM is like an army of protectors defending you against antigens (invaders like viruses, bacteria, and germs). These protectors are called ANTiBODieS, and they are a protein in your blood produced to fight against unwelcome invaders. The way antibodies do this is by roaming around in your bloodstream on the lookout for any foreign substances. When they find an enemy, the antibodies chemically bind to the invader and neutralize them. Hooray!

But what happens if your antibodies think your own cells are invaders?

Nevertheless, despite the pain, exhaustion, and high blood pressure she experienced, Selena continued working.

She starred in a number of films, recorded the voice of Mavis for *Hotel Transylvania 2,* signed with a new record label, and released another album in which she cowrote twelve of the sixteen tracks.

Revival came out in 2015 and was highly praised, receiving many positive reviews. The album was said to reflect her journey since 2013, including the media scrutiny of her personal life and mental health concerns.

"I'm very confident in this record, and you can hear it," Selena said in an interview. "But I'm vulnerable, I'm real, and I think it just shows a different side of me, and I'm really excited, and I feel like a huge weight has been lifted off my shoulders."

In another interview, Selena explained the self-reflective nature of her record. "This is the next phase in my life, and I think it is important for me to take control over it. [Fans] can expect a lot of insight on my perception of things. I think it shows a lot, not just about love."

In 2016 Selena embarked on a concert tour to promote *Revival*.

"I am ready to get back on the road and see my fans in person! This album marks a new and very important chapter in my life. I cannot wait to get onstage and perform this new material."

The tour began in Las Vegas, the Entertainment Capital of the World. On May 6, 2016, Selena stepped onto the stage at Mandalay Bay Events Center.

Lights!

Camera!

Action!

She was greeted by the roar of thousands of adoring fans, in a shower of colorful lights. This would be the first of forty-one concerts Selena gave in cities across North America. The second leg of her tour began in Jakarta, Indonesia, and ended in Tokyo, Japan. In August 2016

Selena was in Melbourne, Australia, and ended the third leg of her tour in Auckland, New Zealand.

In the span of just three months, Selena gave fifty-five concerts across three continents. She still had thirty-six more concerts to give in Asia and Europe. But by the end of August, it was clear that something was very wrong with Selena's health, and she could no longer ignore it.

"I want to be proactive and focus on maintaining my health," she said in an interview, where she explained that she would be canceling the remainder of her tour.

"As many of you know, around a year ago I revealed that I have lupus, an illness that can affect people in different ways. I've discovered that anxiety, panic attacks, and depression can be side effects of lupus, which can present their own challenges."

Selena knew her fans would be incredibly disappointed. She thanked them for being so supportive but also encouraged them to be honest with themselves about their own struggles. She wanted to be a role model for them, showing them how important it was to get help when you are struggling.

"Thank you to all my fans for your support," she said. "You know how special you are to me, but I need to face this head-on to ensure I am doing everything possible to be my best. I know I am not alone by sharing this. I hope others will be encouraged to address their own issues."

Everything came to a halt for Selena.

In August 2016 Selena checked herself into a mental health facility to get treatment for her anxiety, panic attacks, and depression. She made the very brave choice of stepping out of the spotlight and turned her attention instead to caring for her mind and body.

"I had to stop because I had everything, and I was absolutely broken inside," she told her fans. "I kept it all together enough to where I would never let you down, but I kept it too much together to where I let myself down. If you are broken, you do not have to stay broken."

CHAPTER THREE

DIAGNOSIS

"It feels like a sisterhood, and I was just blown away to hear [Selena and Francia] talk."

—SAVANNAH GUTHRIE, TODAY cohost

As Selena had shared with her fans, her mental health had been greatly impacted by her medical condition and the fact that, in a very real way, her body had become its own enemy. It was very stressful to be living with an autoimmune disease that made her body attack itself. To make matters worse, the antibodies in Selena's immune system perceived everything—even what was actually good and healthy—as a threat, and because those antibodies were trying to do their job so well, they had begun to shut down some of Selena's organs.

After undergoing many tests, Selena was diagnosed

with lupus arthritis, one of the most common complications of lupus, causing severe inflammation and a lot of pain. Her kidneys were also struggling. Selena could no longer ignore the situation.

She decided to undergo chemotherapy. Chemotherapy is a treatment (a therapy) of a disease through the use of certain and powerful chemicals. These strong chemicals are designed to weaken the immune system so that it doesn't continue attacking the healthy body. Imagine how strong the chemicals need to be to attack a whole army of protectors.

To your body, it feels as if it's being poisoned. As a result, many patients who go through chemotherapy experience difficult side effects such as nausea, vomiting, diarrhea, exhaustion, and headaches. Also, a weakened immune system means the antibodies that are supposed to shield you against actual foreign invaders, like viruses, are unable to do so. As a result, you are now even more likely to get sick.

Patients going through chemotherapy are in a very fragile situation. It was a scary time for Selena and her loved ones. Unfortunately, this was not the end of her troubles. Things were about to get worse.

Selena's kidneys could no longer function properly, and they began to fail.

Kidneys play a critical role in the body. They act as our

WHAT IS DIALYSIS?

The word $DIALYSIS$ comes from the Greek word διάλυσις, which means "dissolution." In medical terms, dialysis is the process of removing excess water and toxins from a patient's blood in people whose kidneys can no longer perform that function naturally. Dialysis is a temporary solution, usually while patients await a kidney transplant.

filtering system, removing wastes and controlling blood pressure. Most people are born with two kidneys, but only one well-functioning kidney is needed to be healthy. If both kidneys fail, the patient will need dialysis or a kidney transplant to stay alive.

Selena was added to a kidney-transplant list. But the average wait for a new kidney can be up to ten years, and it's a very complicated process. Getting a new kidney isn't just about finding someone who is willing to donate one of their two kidneys. It also needs to be an exact match to your body so that your body doesn't reject the new kidney, thinking it's a foreign object. This is an extremely difficult thing to find.

Selena's situation was becoming dire. Not only could she no longer do the work she loved, but her life was on the line.

Selena was initially very private about her struggle with lupus. Only her family and doctors were aware of the severity of her condition. Fortunately, Selena's friend and roommate at the time, Francia Raísa, knew Selena well enough to understand that her friend was suffering in silence.

Francia was a fellow actress and Disney darling. She and Selena had met in 2013 at a Disney children's hospital visit and, as Francia said, they "just clicked." The two had been "forever friends" since then.

One day, when Selena came home, Francia noticed Selena was particularly exhausted, struggling to even open a water bottle.

"I hadn't asked anything," Francia said in an interview. "I knew that she hadn't been feeling well. She couldn't open a water bottle one day. She chucked it, and she started crying, and I said, 'What's wrong?' and that's when she told me."

So, Francia did what all good friends do, and she created a space for Selena to be vulnerable and share her concerns. When Selena confessed her struggles with lupus, Francia immediately volunteered to be tested as a possible kidney donor.

"It was something I could never ask someone to do,"

Selena confessed in an interview. But Francia didn't need to be asked. She wasted no time in doing the blood work and undergoing the required medical testing. This included making sure that Francia was not only physically healthy but also mentally and emotionally sound. After all, this was a very emotionally trying process.

The surgery was not without risk for Francia. Having a kidney removed is a serious operation with frightening long-term consequences. Living without a kidney also puts the donor at great risk of complications as they age. In addition to the physical impact on Francia's body, she would have to put her career on hold until she recovered from the surgery, a long and painful process.

This was not an easy decision for Francia to make, or one without lifelong implications for the young actress. But Francia didn't hesitate, and to everyone's surprise (and immense delight) Francia was a perfect match!

"The fact that she was a match," Selena said, shaking her head. "I mean, that's unbelievable. That's not real."

The day they found out that Francia was a match, Francia gave Selena a gift: It was a box she had custom-made, with an engraving at the top that read "A sister is a forever friend." Inside the box she placed a kidney bean, a token of her deep love and commitment to her "sister."

Things moved quickly after that; time was running out for Selena.

So, one early morning in the summer of 2017, Francia and Selena arrived at the hospital to begin the organ donation process. Francia went into surgery first to have one of her kidney's removed.

Beep

Beep

Beep

Selena and Francia's family waited anxiously to hear that the surgery went well.

And it did. Francia woke up feeling very peaceful and calm. She asked to see Selena before Selena went in for surgery. The friends held hands.

"We're doing this."

It was then Selena's turn.

Beep

Beep

Beep

Two hours later, Selena woke up. She felt fine, saw her mom and stepdad, and told Francia she loved her. But as she tried to get some rest, Selena began to hyperventilate. Something was not right.

"I started to attempt to fall asleep," Selena said, "and in the middle of that process, I started hyperventilating and there was so much pain. My teeth were grinding; I was freaking out."

This was not expected, and Selena was terrified. The doctors quickly discovered that her new kidney had turned around and broken one of her arteries.

Emergency!

Selena was once again wheeled into surgery.

Beep

Beep

Beep

For six long and stressful hours, the doctors worked on Selena. Patiently and carefully, they guided her kidney back into place. Because the artery had broken, they had to remove a vein from her leg and build a new artery to keep her kidney in place.

Beep

Beep

Beep

Selena's life was very much on the line. Fortunately the surgery was a success.

After the second operation, Selena was utterly exhausted. Her body was drained of all energy. But she was grateful to be alive, and especially for Francia's lifesaving gift.

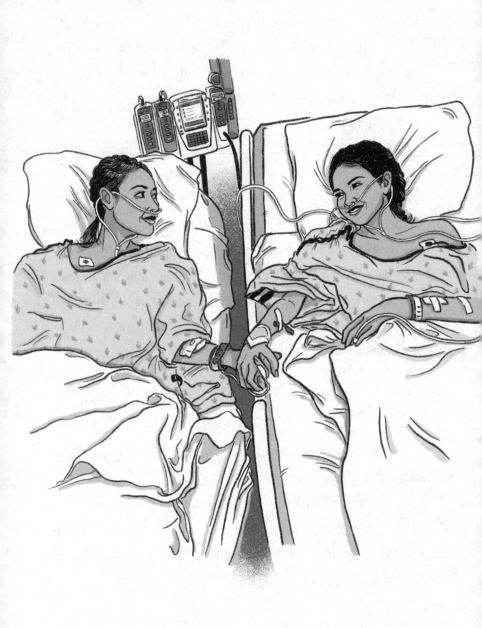

The recovery would take time for both Selena and Francia. Selena wanted to be with her sister and forever friend through it all. So she found a space for her and Francia to heal together. They were on bed rest, allowed to walk only an hour a day. They constantly needed to ask for help, even to do the most ordinary things like getting dressed. They couldn't even shower on their own.

"It was a very humbling experience," Francia said in an interview. But it's one that both Francia and Selena are grateful for. To their immense relief, Selena's symptoms fell away and her body began to recover.

"It's really hard to think about or even to swallow," Selena said, "especially now, that as soon as I got the kidney transplant, my arthritis went away; my lupus, there's about a three to five percent chance it'll ever come back; my blood pressure is better; my energy, my life has been better."

Despite the arduous journey and how private Selena was, she knew this was an opportunity to raise awareness about the importance of kidney donations but also about the importance of allowing others to help you when you most need a friend.

So Selena and Francia decided to share their story, to show how something as terrifying as this life-and-death experience could have a positive impact on them and hopefully others.

"I just really hope that we can help somebody," Selena said. "I really do. I don't think what we went through was easy, I don't think it was fun. I just hope this inspires people to feel good and to know that there are really good people in the world."

After her surgery, Selena helped raise almost $500,000 for lupus research through her fans and social media platform.

"There aren't words to describe how I can possibly

thank my beautiful friend Francia Raísa," Selena said in an Instagram post. "She gave me the ultimate gift and sacrifice by donating her kidney to me. I am incredibly blessed. Lupus continues to be very misunderstood, but progress is being made. For more information regarding lupus please go to the Lupus Research Alliance website: www.lupusresearch.org."

CHAPTER FOUR

BOUNCING BACK

"Gomez re-enters public life with grace and
clarity, two very rare finds indeed."

—BRITTANY SPANOS, *Rolling Stone*

With her inner strength returning, Selena's passion for making art also returned with fervor.

"I stopped, and then I continued, because I realized that I needed to challenge myself," she said. "Do I really love this? Is this worth it anymore? I would look at my crowd on tour and think, *Yes, this is worth it, right?*"

Selena began working on musical collaborations with various songwriters and producers. She recorded new songs and music videos. She was cast in a number of films. Selena even flexed her executive producer muscles on a Netflix series adaptation of Jay Asher's novel *Thirteen Reasons Why.*

But being in the spotlight all the time continued to be exhausting.

"Growing up is frustrating," Selena said, "because you are a kid and figuring out your life. And everyone is watching and speculating. People will pick apart everything."

And that was very true.

All aspects of Selena's life were closely observed by millions of followers and critics; every big or little thing she did or said or wore or ate was always under scrutiny; her choices, her art, her life were constantly criticized on the social media stage. As a result, Selena was always comparing herself to the image people had of her, the person others wanted her to be.

"I can't meet someone and know if they like me for me," she said in an interview. "I just want to start over. I want everything to be brand-new. I want someone to love me like I'm brand-new."

But she wasn't brand-new—she was a huge international brand. Social media began to take over her life as she worked so hard to curate her real self to match the social media presence.

"Instagram became my whole world, and it was really dangerous," she said. "It's what I woke up to and went to sleep to. I was an addict, and it felt like I was seeing things I didn't want to see. I would look at myself in the mirror and I just felt like *I've had enough; I don't know if I can go on anymore.*"

But she was so passionate about her work and connecting with her fans that she couldn't imagine stepping away from that. Instead, she kept pushing herself to do more, to be more. And all the while, everything she did was closely scrutinized, critically analyzed, mercilessly picked apart.

Until . . .

"I woke up one morning and looked at Instagram, like every other person, and I was done. I was tired of reading horrible things. My self-esteem was shot," she said in an interview. "I started to have panic attacks right before getting onstage, or right after leaving the stage. Basically I felt I wasn't good enough, wasn't capable. I felt I wasn't giving my fans anything, and they could see it—which, I think, was a complete distortion."

It seemed Selena had lost perspective.

She had been so focused on what everyone else said about her—that she had lost all faith in herself.

Broken and dismayed, Selena knew the only way out was to regain that trust; to look in the mirror and see the strength she knew she had inside.

So Selena made a life-changing decision: She was going to take control of her mental health, committing once and for all to healing. The first step was breaking her social media addiction.

Swipe

Click

Selena turned off her phone and set aside her devices.

She shut off the voices clamoring for her attention on the outside, giving the voices whispering on the inside a chance to be heard, to remind her of who *she* was: someone who cares deeply about others and needed to care deeply about herself, too.

"Taking a break from social media was the best decision that I've ever made for my mental health," Selena said. "I created a system where I still don't have my passwords."

Selena asked her personal assistant to manage her social media accounts, posting content and monitoring her platforms.

"And the unnecessary hate and comparisons went away once I put my phone down."

The relief was immense.

"I'll have moments where that weird feeling will come back," Selena said, "but now I have a much better relationship with myself. After that decision, it was instant freedom. My life in front of me was my life, and I was present, and I could not have been more happy about it."

Selena knew she had made the right choice, but she was hesitant to share her social media addiction and struggles publicly at first. As her social media platforms clearly demonstrated, she had an amazing life, and she was extremely grateful for all of it. It was hard to explain why she was suffering so much.

"I feel guilty for my position a lot," Selena said in an interview.

Of course, she had worked hard for what she had. After all, she had grown up in poverty. She had certainly earned her success and built up her brand through her own efforts. Nevertheless, she had so much now, where others had so little. How could she possibly complain?

Moreover, Selena knew that sharing her struggles would publicize her vulnerability, show the world that she was not as rock-solid as everyone thought. What would everyone say? The media would pounce on her; they would analyze and criticize her to no end.

But Selena knew very well that she was not alone in her suffering. Thousands, perhaps millions, of adoring fans shared her pain, and Selena realized that she could use her position to help others going through similar struggles.

"I became aware that my little world is complicated, but the picture is much bigger than the stuff I deal with," she said.

There were so many other children who felt as she did, suffering with self-esteem issues, loss of trust, depression, and anxiety. Those children needed to know that they were not alone; that even their superstars felt vulnerable and afraid. They needed to know that it was okay for them to feel that way, too.

So Selena took the brave step of choosing to go public with her story. But not just sharing it. Selena chose to use this as an opportunity to reframe the entire narrative around mental health, making it a major part of her brand moving forward.

Selena once again used her massive platform and fan base to raise awareness, this time about mental health.

She wanted to encourage children to be more open about their struggles, with themselves and loved ones. By very deliberately choosing not to hide from the truth of this pain, she gave her fans and followers a space to open up and accept their own truths, whatever they may be.

"My lupus, my kidney transplant, chemotherapy, having a mental illness, going through very public heartbreaks—these were all things that honestly should have taken me down," she said. "Every time I went through something, I was like, *What else? What else am I going to have to deal with?*"

And every time she had to deal with something new, she didn't hide it from her fans. Nor did she hide the fact that she was not going to let these blows knock her down. Instead, Selena used her platform and brand to show how those experiences helped her learn, grow, and transform.

"That's really what kept me going," she said.

During a time when she did not feel strong enough to take care of herself, she found strength in finding ways of caring for others. Just like she had as a young girl in preschool or helping out at soup kitchens with her mom.

"I'm just so passionate about that, and I think I will

continue to be for the rest of my life," she said. "Especially since the COVID-19 pandemic, there are so many people I know who craved help but had no idea how to get it. I have big aspirations for that field and really want to implement more education behind it."

Once Selena took her mental health seriously, she received an official diagnosis of anxiety, depression, and bipolar disorder. Bipolar disorder is a mental health condition that causes extreme mood swings in patients.

"My highs were really high," Selena said, "and my lows would take me out for weeks at a time." It was stressful and confusing because she didn't know what was happening.

"I felt a huge weight lifted off me when I found out," she shared in an interview. "I could take a deep breath and go, 'Okay, that explains so much.'"

Selena began working closely with a therapist, trying to identify and ultimately change patterns of negative thinking into positive behaviors, using a method called dialectic behavioral therapy. One of the key principles of dialectic behavioral therapy is learning to accept your experience, to be honest with yourself about your struggles. Selena took this to heart and decided to be completely open with her friends and loyal fans about her mental health struggles.

"Once I stopped and accepted my vulnerability and decided to share my story with people—that's when I felt release," she said.

The second component of dialectic behavioral therapy is about change: recognizing the negative forces pushing against you and actively working to develop more positive coping strategies.

"It's a lonely journey to really figure out where all this stuff is coming from. And to detach from it," Selena said. "It becomes a habit, retraining your mind to not go to these negative places when you say something wrong, do something wrong, when you wear a certain thing or represent a certain culture."

For example, when Selena realized her addiction to social media was a big part of where all the negativity was coming from, she engaged the help of her friends and family to help her manage the amount of time she spent on the platforms, the content that was posted, and what she actually paid attention to.

She also focused on self-reflection, training herself to be aware of how she was treating herself and others.

"There are moments where I just have to center myself and let the thoughts come in. Sometimes I'll write them down and then completely just sit with *What is it?*

What is the root of this? Why can I get to the bottom of this? And it really helps me."

Throughout this journey, Selena came to a very important realization: She had always wanted to be part of something great, and yet her whole life people had made her feel like she was not good enough to be great. But the truth was, she *was* good enough. What she had to learn was to trust herself, to believe that she was exactly who she was supposed to be, despite what anybody else said.

Slowly, Selena began to rebuild herself.

In 2019, Selena released "Lose You to Love Me," a single from her third solo studio album, *Rare*.

I needed to lose you to find me . . .
I needed to hate you to love me, yeah

"Lose You to Love Me" was a love letter Selena wrote to herself, a manifesto for all to hear: She was no longer going to sacrifice who she was, her dreams, her aspirations, her purpose. Selena wasn't going to let others dictate who she was. She was in control.

The day after she released "Lose You to Love Me," Selena released a second single from her album, this one titled "Look at Her Now."

Took a few years to soak up the tears
But look at her now, watch her go

As the lyrics of "Look at Her Now" demonstrate, this is a song about empowerment, about recognizing your vulnerability and not letting it bring you down.

With these two songs, Selena finally reclaimed the person she always knew she was but had forgotten along the way.

And her fans loved her for it.

"Lose You to Love Me" became Selena's first number-one single in the United States, skyrocketing to the top of the Billboard Hot 100. Her album *Rare* was released later that year and debuted at the top of the Billboard 200.

"You inspire me to be better," a confident Selena told her fans. And she thanked them because *they* had believed in her throughout the years, even when she hadn't believed in herself.

This empowered self-reflection helped Selena remember the core values that had always grounded her: empathy, thoughtfulness, fearlessness. She became a strident and vocal advocate for kindness, reminding fans and followers that words have power, that negative comments can have great influence, and that positive support can change lives.

In 2020, Selena launched Rare Beauty, a cosmetic collection focusing on embracing one's natural beauty and rejecting the unrealistic standards of perfection.

"I've spent years of my life trying to look like other people," she said in an interview. "I would see an image, and I would be like, *My gosh, why don't I look like that?* None of that was good for me."

Now, Selena was done with that. Instead, she wanted people to know they were special, to see that they were worthy just as they were. For her, makeup isn't something you use to change yourself. It is an art form you use to complement your natural beauty.

"Beauty is a part of your self-esteem, how you see yourself."

And not just on the outside but on the inside as well.

Selena collaborated on the creation of Mental Health 101, a tool kit of resources that can be found on her Rare Beauty website. Her company also has a charitable arm, Rare Impact Fund, with the aim of raising $100 million over the next ten years to help improve access to mental health resources.

"Everything that I'm attached to has a charity aspect," she said in an interview. "If something good isn't coming out of it, I'm not going to do it. I don't need money. I need people who want to fight with me."

And that fight is to do good, to be a voice for others who don't know what's going on or what they're feeling; to say the things that others are afraid to say; to remind us all that we can stand up for what we care about, that we don't need to live in fear of our own vulnerability.

It was this very courage to speak for those who are silent that brought Selena one of her most ambitious projects yet.

CHAPTER FIVE

GIVING BACK

"I've met thousands of people in my life,
and I wish that they can see what I see [in] them."

—Selena Gomez

Hidden in the back of a truck, shrouded in darkness and silence, a woman held her breath as the truck rolled over the bumpy road crossing the dusty border between Mexico

and the United States. It was the 1970s, and the woman was Selena's aunt. Years later Selena's grandparents followed. In 1992, Selena's father was born in the United States. But despite being an American citizen, his Mexican heritage made him a constant target of racism and hate speech.

"Growing up, we didn't have much," Selena said, "and we were treated poorly. My dad would get pulled over all the time, and he wasn't doing anything most of the time."

But they were afraid to speak up.

"It's just going to stir up more trouble for me, not them," her father told her.

The United States as we know it today was shaped by immigrants who came from all over the world in search of hope and better opportunities.

As John F. Kennedy famously said, "Every American who has ever lived, with the exception of one group, was either an immigrant himself or a descendant of immigrants."

The contributions of immigrants have been invaluable, making the United States one of the most powerful and bountiful countries in the world.

For example: Levi Strauss (immigrated in 1847) changed the course of fashion when he invented Levi's jeans. John Muir (immigrated in 1849) helped preserve many of the United States' natural treasures and helped establish

Yosemite National Park. Joseph Pulitzer (immigrated in 1864) established modern American journalism as we know it. Nikola Tesla (immigrated in 1884) was an engineer and scientist who devised the electrical system used across the world today. Albert Einstein (immigrated in the 1930s) was a mathematician, inventor, and physicist who developed the theory of relativity, among other significant scientific accomplishments. Madeleine Albright (immigrated in 1948) was the first female secretary of state in the United States. Gloria Estefan (immigrated in 1959) is an internationally acclaimed singer, actress, and businesswoman, celebrated as one of the greatest Latinx artists of all time. Sergey Brin (immigrated in the 1970s), an inventor and engineer, cofounded Google.

And these are just a few of thousands of accomplished immigrants who have made the United States the wonderful nation it is.

But think about how difficult it must be to immigrate to another country.

First, a person must prove that they have a good reason for wanting to immigrate. Each country has specific guidelines about what counts as a valid justification for entry, but that country's government may not agree with its immigrants on what is and isn't a good reason.

Second, immigrants need to demonstrate that they are

law-abiding citizens in their homeland and will follow the rules of the new country. They have to provide a lot of documents about their education, their employment, and anything that might help support their case for being good and law-abiding citizens of the new country.

Some people may also need a sponsor, someone in the new country who will agree to take responsibility for them. The sponsor will be asked to prove that they can take care of you, that they are a law-abiding citizen, and that there is a good reason for wanting to sponsor an immigrant.

Once all immigration application and sponsorship documents have been submitted, the case can be reviewed. This can take many months, sometimes years! A potential immigrant and their sponsor may be asked to provide additional information or clarification about some of the things they said.

If all the paperwork is approved, they need to go to an interview where government officials will ask many questions about the person's current situation and their future plans. Assuming the interview goes well and all the paperwork is in order, a person may be granted permission to immigrate.

Immigration is a complicated and long-drawn-out process.

In the United States there are many rules and regulations. Because so many people want to immigrate to the United States, there is also a long wait, and quite often, things fall behind. The US immigration system is also outdated, and it needs to address new situations that were not considered when it was first devised.

Beyond the extensive, yearslong process to become an immigrant in the United States, there are also considerable barriers, including language and communication, as well as the cost of the applications and immigration lawyers. Additionally, with a non-permanent immigration status—that is, people who enter the country on a temporary, or short-term, basis—it's nearly impossible to secure proper work and housing for themselves, and much less their families.

Even more, all these processes and their uncertainty can inflict mental strain on immigrants, many of whom live in constant fear of deportation and separation from their families by regulating authorities, causing undue psychological stress and trauma. As a result, the topic of immigration has become the subject of many political arguments and controversial news stories.

"But immigration goes beyond politics and headlines," Selena said. "It is a human issue, affecting real people, dismantling real lives. How we deal with it speaks to our humanity, our empathy, our compassion. How we treat our fellow human beings defines who we are."

In 2019, Selena announced that she would be producing

the Netflix docuseries *Living Undocumented,* a six-episode series following eight undocumented families in the United States as they navigated the complex US immigration system.

LIVING | UNDOCUMENTED

"I chose to produce this series because over the past few years, the word *immigrant* has seemingly become a negative word," Selena said in an interview. "My hope is that the series can shed light on what it's like to live in this country as an undocumented immigrant firsthand, from the courageous people who have chosen to share their stories."

Selena wanted to humanize the stories of people who had been reduced to basic headlines, once again using her powerful platform to promote the values she deemed most important: kindness, empathy, and fearlessness. She wanted to speak out against misinformation and hate speech, to raise awareness about the very real dangers of human trafficking and the harrowing challenges faced by undocumented immigrants.

Selena shared details of her experience meeting with three of the young people documented in the series,

including Bar, a Dreamer whose family fled Israel when she was just six months old.

"Bar told me she wanted to study interior design," Selena said. "She also told me that she's lived in fear her whole life. A week before we met, she had been violently robbed but was afraid to call the police. She didn't want them to discover that her parents are undocumented and report them to ICE."

That fear spoke to Selena. "It captured the shame, uncertainty, and fear I saw my own family struggle with."

And then there were Pablo and Camilo Dunoyer, brothers who fled Colombia in 2002 to escape the narco-guerillas who were threatening their family.

DREAMERS

A DREAMER is the term used for children who are protected by the Development, Relief, and Education for Alien Minors Act (knows as the DREAM Act). Dreamers are children who were brought to the United States as minor saccompanying undocumented immigrants. The program grants them temporary residency and the chance to attain permanent residency if they satisfy certain qualifications.

WHAT IS ICE?

The US IMMIGRATION AND CUSTOMS ENFORCEMENT (ICE) is a federal law enforcement agency under the US Department of Homeland Security. Their stated mission is to secure the borders of the United States against cross-border crime and illegal immigration.

ICE has two primary law enforcement components: Homeland Security Investigations (HSI) and Enforcement and Removal Operations (ERO). ERO is the office that handles deportation of undocumented noncitizens, and maintains custodial facilities used to detain people who are illegally present in the United States.

Pablo was a great student, hardworking and dedicated. He was accepted to San Diego State University, but he couldn't go. That summer, his father had been detained by immigration services and held in a cage with other immigrants.

"They slept on the floor with aluminum blankets for warmth," Selena said. "The lights stayed on at all hours of the day. Pablo said he'd never heard pain like that in his father's voice, and he's worried he will carry that pain for the rest of his life."

After eight terrifying days, Pablo's father was deported and sent back to Colombia, where his family had received death threats. Pablo and Camilo had to go into hiding, afraid they, too, would be picked up and sent back to the violence they fought so hard to escape. The brothers could no longer go home, and they had a hard time sleeping, knowing their time was running out.

But even despite their fear of deportation, Camilo confessed to fearing something even more.

"His biggest fear," Selena said, "is being forgotten and becoming another faceless statistic."

Selena felt a great responsibility, not only as a Mexican American but as someone with a deep capacity for empathy and compassion, to use her voice and her platform for those who were too afraid to speak.

"And I hope that getting to know these eight families and their stories will inspire people to be more compassionate, and to learn more about immigration and form their own opinion. I hope that Bar gets to study interior design. I hope that Pablo and Camilo can return home and sleep at night."

Of course, elevating the voices of undocumented immigrants did not come without its staunch criticism. But that did not dissuade Selena from doing what she thought was right.

"The truth is, the worst criticism I can imagine is still nothing compared to what undocumented immigrants face every day. Fear shouldn't stop us from getting involved and educating ourselves on an issue that affects millions of people in our country. Fear didn't stop my aunt from getting into the back of that truck. And for that, I will always be grateful."

Immigration is not the only social issue that Selena is passionate about.

In 2009, at the age of seventeen, Selena was appointed UNICEF ambassador, the youngest appointee at that time. In this role Selena would use her voice, her brand, and her international recognition to help fundraise, educate, and advocate for support of the organization's mission to help reduce preventable deaths in children.

UNICEF, also known as the UNITED NATIONS INTERNATIONAL CHILDREN'S EMERGENCY FUND, is a United Nations agency responsible for humanitarian and developmental aid to children around the world. With offices in more than 150 countries, UNICEF provides children with clean water, healthy food, education, emergency aid, and medical assistance.

Despite being one of the largest and most impactful humanitarian organizations in the world, more than twenty-five thousand children still die every day from preventable causes.

"I stand with UNICEF in the belief that we can change that number from twenty-five thousand to zero," Selena said when she was appointed ambassador. "I know we can achieve this because every moment, UNICEF is on the ground providing children with the lifesaving assistance needed to ensure zero becomes a reality."

Her first official field mission was to Ghana, where Selena witnessed firsthand the devastating consequences on children of malnutrition and lack of adequate health care and education.

"It was completely life-changing and eye-opening," Selena said.

That year, she raised $700,000 for the UNICEF campaign and continued to be an ambassador for two more years. Even after her role as ambassador ended, Selena remained actively involved with the organization, participating in a celebrity auction and returning as UNICEF spokesperson for the organization's sixtieth anniversary. Selena Gomez & the Scene even staged a reunion, holding a benefit concert at the sixtieth anniversary and donating all proceeds to the UNICEF campaign.

In 2011 Selena traveled to Chile in connection with the UNICEF-supported Programa Puente, set up to help families better understand child education and development.

"UNICEF is helping Chilean families get out of poverty, prevent violence within the home, and promote education. To witness firsthand these families' struggles, and also their hope and perseverance, was truly inspiring."

THE REPUBLIC
OF GHANA

GHANA (officially called the Republic of Ghana) is a country in western Africa on the coast of the Gulf of Guinea. Despite being relatively small in size and population compared to other African nations, it is one of the leading countries in Africa because of its natural wealth: lush forests, diverse animal life (including lions, leopards, and elephants), and miles of coastline. Cacao (the bean used to make chocolate) is one of its main exports but so are gold and diamonds.

More than thirty-one million people live in Ghana, many of them suffering in abject poverty.

Selena's philanthropic involvement didn't end with UNICEF. She has been involved with various charities raising awareness on issues of social justice, environmental friendly behavior, and animal protection.

She also began to use her platform to speak out on major social issues. For instance, in 2017 Selena participated in *Billboard*'s 30 Days of Pride, writing love letters in support of the LGBTQ+ community.

"I remember as a young child going to brunch on Sundays with my mom and her group of friends," she wrote. "I had no idea they were all gay as I didn't even comprehend what that meant at the time. All I knew is that I loved being surrounded by these kind, fun, and loving friends my mother had around her. I definitely give credit to her for raising me in an environment that was incredibly open-minded and nonjudgmental . . .

"There is still a significant amount of work to do," she added in her letter. "And I look forward to the day when a person is never judged, discriminated, or feared for their sexuality."

And her advocacy went beyond penning beautiful words. The year prior, Selena actively protested against the "bathroom bill" in North Carolina (known as HB2), donating proceeds from her show to LGBTQ+-supporting charities.

WHAT IS HOUSE
BILL 2 (HB2)?

HB2 was a bill signed into law in North Carolina in 2016. The law required that individuals in government buildings must use restrooms that corresponded to the gender listed on their birth certificate rather than the gender they identified with. The law was very controversial and met with fierce opposition by people who feared it would allow discrimination against the LGBTQ+ community. Portions of the law were later repealed in 2017 in North Carolina. However, many state legislatures have proposed similar bills that would restrict public bathroom access on the basis of sex as biologically defined.

"I am very fortunate to have grown up in a home where I learned from an early age that everyone should be treated equally," she said at the time. "I feel like my generation is the most progressive one yet and believe there will be a day soon when laws like HB2 won't even be a consideration."

Selena has also been a strong supporter of the Black Lives Matter movement.

In 2020, as protests erupted across the country in response to violence against the Black community, Selena invited Alicia Garza, cofounder of the Black Lives Matter movement, to temporarily take over her account in order to reach millions of followers directly.

"I have been struggling to know the right things to say to get the word out about this important moment in history," Selena told her fans. "After thinking about how best to use my social media, I decided that we all need to hear more from Black voices. Over the next few days I will be highlighting influential leaders and giving them a chance to take over my Instagram so that they can speak directly to all of us. We all have an obligation to do better, and we can start by listening with an open heart and mind."

Alicia Garza posted a video on Gomez's account in which she shared the following message:

"So look, there's a lot happening in our country right now . . . here's the deal: People are in the streets right now, because Black people are being murdered by police, and police are not being held accountable. This is a big, big problem. Everybody is taught that if you do

BLACK LIVES
MATTER

The BLACK LIVES MATTER movement was founded in 2013 in response to the acquittal of Trayvon Martin's murderer. According to their website: "Black Lives Matter Global Network Foundation, Inc. is a global organization in the United States, the United Kingdom, and Canada, whose mission is to eradicate white supremacy and build local power to intervene in violence inflicted on Black communities by the state and vigilantes. By combating and countering acts of violence, creating space for Black imagination and innovation, and centering Black joy, we are winning immediate improvements in our lives."

something wrong, you have to make it right. And when it comes to Black folks and police, there is a dynamic where Black people are being murdered, sometimes on camera, sometimes not by police, and police are not having to make it right. Huge problem in this country. We've seen it time and time again for decades and decades and decades, and people are sick and tired of being sick and tired. Well, I am also sick and tired of being sick and tired, which is why I work in an organization that works to organize Black communities and train our communities to change the rules that allow police officers to not be accountable when they do bad things in our communities."

But Selena's goal was not just to share her platform in order to amplify Black voices. She wanted this to be an opportunity to educate her fans as well.

"Educating ourselves is the first step if we hope to make any progress in bringing an end to systemic racism," she posted. "As much as one might want to believe things have gotten better, we cannot deny any longer that they have not."

Her drive to raise awareness and educate her followers extended into other key social issues such as voting.

"At first it was just me educating people on the voting

process," she said, but then she became involved with the organization When We All Vote, an initiative created by Michelle Obama to help educate, engage, and empower voters.

Once again, Selena lent her Instagram account and massive social media following to activists and philanthropists helping to keep voters informed and aware of their rights.

Selena's drive to educate and empower extends to her ongoing campaign against misinformation and hate speech. For the past few years, Selena has become a vocal critic of social media companies and how their platforms are used to sow despair and animosity, low self-esteem, and a mental health crisis.

But she is also using her voice to empower young people to take care of themselves and one another; to stay true to who they are and what they believe.

"If you're doing something you love, do it because you love it and believe you can do it."

This is the truth Selena has always believed, despite struggling to hold on to it at times. And in the end, that is what Selena's story is really about—learning to believe in yourself and having the courage to live that truth.

Recently Selena said, "I haven't even touched the surface of what I want to do," and one can't help but know it's true.

As she dives into a new role as executive producer of *Selena + Chef*, which airs on HBO Max, Selena reveals a new and vulnerable side of herself, but one that she is not afraid to explore.

"I've always been very vocal about my love of food," she said in an interview. "I think I've been asked hundreds of times . . . if I had another career, what would I do, and I've answered that it would be fun to be a chef. I definitely don't have the formal training, though! Like many of us, while being home, I find myself cooking more and experimenting in the kitchen."

It is in this fearlessness that her true power lies.

As Andy Forssell, the head of HBO Max, recently explained, "Blending her determination with top-tier culinary artists is sure to entertain and educate viewers about something we're all trying to work through—how to make cooking at home exciting, fun, and delicious."

Selena is also starring in and executive producing an exciting new mystery comedy series with acting legends Steve Martin and Martin Short. *Only Murders in the Building* premiered in 2021 and is her first scripted television series since her days on *Wizards of Waverly Place*. Selena has come a long way from her early days on set!

In 2020 *Time* magazine nominated her as one of the most influential people in the world.

"Selena Gomez is unabashedly spreading her wings and influence into whatever lane her passions lead her," the interview read. "She has always been a great musician, but she's also always been more than her music. Selena courageously uses her global platform in service of her full identity. She is emblematic of her powerful generation, which patently rejects the notion that they belong in any one lane as artists, activists, or citizens of the world."

Flash!

Fame has followed at the heels of that young girl who was photographed at a preschool in Grand Prairie, Texas, so many years ago. And yet, despite its gilded appeal, Selena has not let it distract her from the most important thing.

"You are special," she recently told her fans. "You're supposed to be [exactly] who you are."

DID YOU KNOW?

★ As of the 2020 US Census, Hispanic and Latinx people of any race were 39.3 percent of Texas's population. Texas ranks #2 in total Hispanic population among states in the US.

demographics.texas.gov/Resources/Publications /2021/20211004_HispanicHeritageMonth.pdf

★ Hispanic roots in Texas are unquestionably some of the deepest in the United States—Hispanics were among the original Texans. Indigenous people lived in the area long before Spanish explorers arrived, and a mixture of the two, the mestizos, are the cornerstone of the state. The Hispanic story is a very American story, and you can see it clearly in Texas, where Latinx culture and community have shaped the land.

thc.texas.gov/education/texas-history-home /hispanic-heritage

★ In Texas, one in six residents is an immigrant, while another one in six is born in the United States to at least one immigrant parent. As of 2018, 1.9 million immigrants had naturalized, and 957,647 immigrants were eligible to become US citizens in 2017.

americanimmigrationcouncil.org/research/immigrants-in-texas

★ Representing about 83 percent of the population of Texas with 9.5 million residents, Mexicans make up the largest ethnic group in the state. There are about 100,000 people from each of these other ethnic groups: Salvadorans, Puerto Ricans, Hondurans, and Guatemalans.

demographics.texas.gov/Resources

/Publications/2021/20211004_HispanicHeritageMonth.pdf

★ Hispanic values place family first. 35 percent of Hispanic children have lived in an extended family—that means living with a relative other than their parent or sibling. Just like Selena's childhood.

tandfonline.com/doi/abs/10.1080

/00324728.2018.1468476?journalCode=rpst20

★ Selena Quintanilla is a Latina icon in pop culture. Since her death, she has been commemorated with a statue, a Madame Tussaud's wax figure, several television doc-umentaries, a full-length film biopic starring Jennifer Lopez, and a TV series. She was posthumously hon-ored with a Lifetime Achievement Award at the 2021 Grammys and is still remembered publicly as the Queen of Tejano Music and privately by families who name their children after the singer.

womenshistory.si.edu/spotlight/latin-music-legends-stamps
/selena

★ Disney's original TV shows, movies, and even Broad-way shows had an incredible influence on the 2000s generation, launching the careers of artists like Miley Cyrus, Zac Efron, the Jonas Brothers, and Demi Lovato.

vocal.media/geeks/disneys-deeper-impact

★ *Wizards of Waverly Place*, starring Selena Gomez, is Disney Channel's longest-running original series, and its one-hour series finale became the show's most-watched episode.

hollywoodreporter.com/tv/tv-news/wizards-of-waverly
-place-selena-gomez-279824/

celebrity.fm/what-is-the-longest-running-disney
-channel-show/

★ Selena released her first Spanish-language EP, *Revelación,* in 2021. The album features seven reggaeton- and R&B-influenced tracks, which she prepared for by meeting with a translator and vocal coach since she isn't fluent in the language.

rollingstone.com/music/music-features/selena-gomez
-revelacion-interview-1140695/

texasmonthly.com/arts-entertainment/selena-gomez-shines
-on-her-first-spanish-language-ep/

A NOTE FROM KARLA ARENAS VALENTI

The year 2020 was a difficult one for me and my family as we grappled with a challenging mental health crisis. We witnessed firsthand how quickly things can devolve into devastating consequences if mental health is not taken seriously. Fortunately, we were not afraid to take action and find the resources we needed to weather this storm. Many others are not so lucky. And many don't even know there is help to be found. Which is why raising awareness about these issues is so important and can have a truly powerful impact on people.

This was one of the main reasons I was so excited to join this project. Selena Gomez has built a formidable celebrity brand and platform. She has millions of followers—millions of minds watching, listening, following in her footsteps. With that level of fandom comes a big responsibility, a recognition that one has the power to shape lives. And Selena takes that seriously.

What she has done with her platform is truly admirable—not just raising awareness but letting her fans know that they do not need to be ashamed about mental health challenges or hide their struggles; that they are part of a broader network that sees them as they are and can help keep them afloat. That is no easy feat.

As I researched this brave young woman, my admiration for her grew manifold. Her courage is inspiring and her advocacy empowering. It has been a privilege to be part of this journey, celebrating a truly remarkable Hispanic Star.

A NOTE FROM HISPANIC STAR

When Hispanic Star decided to join Macmillan and Roaring Brook Press in creating this chapter book biography series, our intention was to share stories of incredible Hispanic leaders with young readers, inspiring them through the acts of those Stars. For centuries, the Hispanic community has made significant contributions to different spaces of our collective culture—whether it's sports, entertainment, art, politics, or business—and we wanted to showcase some of the role models who made this possible. We especially wanted to inspire Latinx children to rise up and take the mantle of Hispanic unity and pride.

With Hispanic Star, we also wanted to shine a light on the common language that unifies a large portion of the Latinx community. *Hispanic* means "Spanish speaking" and frequently refers to people whose origins are from a country where Spanish is the primary spoken language. The term *Latinx,* in all its ever-changing deviations, refers to people of all gender identities from all countries in Latin

America and their descendants, many of them already born in the United States.

This groundbreaking book series can be found both in English and Spanish as a tribute to the Hispanic community in our country.

We encourage all of our readers to get to know these heroes and the positive impact they continue to have, inviting future generations to learn more about the different journeys of our unique and charming Hispanic Stars!